FAWN PRESS

Salt & Metal
This edition published in 2022 by Fawn Press. Cover design by
Fawn Press.
Author: Sallyanne Rock
ISBN 978-1-3999-1941-8
Printed and bound by Kingate Press, Birmingham, UK.

"Poetry that takes you by the hand and leads you into the woods"

Sallyanne Rock is from the Black Country. Her poetry has been published in various journals and anthologies including *Eye Flash, Away With Words, Anthropocene, Finished Creatures* and *100 Voices*. Her work has been displayed alongside *The Women's Quilt* at National Trust The Workhouse, Southwell. She was awarded the Creative Future Gold Prize for Poetry in 2019. This is her debut pamphlet.

Praise for 'Salt & Metal'

Sallyanne Rock's collection Salt & Metal is a surgical incision into dark hearted and visceral poetry. The poems are voices from a one sided conversation; an internal scream perhaps or the song left falling through the air when a mouth is slammed shut. These poems are brutal, but vulnerable, with a close attention to texture and craft and a voice that doesn't shy away from the truth. One that I will return to. -**Wendy Pratt**

In multi-faceted poems that '*Lift out the heart with one hand / and slice it like a bread roll*' Sallyanne Rock shines a blazing light on assault and domestic abuse. These are important poems, resonant and vital; not always comfortable to read, but exquisitely crafted, with skilfully controlled imagery and an unerring ear for linguistic precision. Rock uses the alchemical properties of poetry to transform experience to testimony, refusing to be defined by the actions of others, and ultimately finding strength in reclamation of both self and home. - **Sarah Doyle**

The first poem's opening line springs a trap and Rock sets out with keen eye and ear, and impressive formal range, to map the trap's dimensions. In violence and ugliness, beauty survives, nurtured by a lyrical gift. What results is a lamplight, sometimes painfully bright, exposing the trap's jagged contours. But more important than this, the light beams out like a flare in the sky, or a firework to celebrate, to say 'screw you, we're free now, we're still here'. - **Liam Bates**

These poems show great strength in all their vulnerability. They are unflinching yet cautious, brutal yet tender, beautiful in their sadness. Salt & Metal shines a light on the struggle, pain and complexities of domestic abuse whilst singing of hope, resurrection and ultimately survival. I loved every word. -**Maria Ferguson**

I read Sallyanne Rock's Salt and Metal, reflecting on a dark period of domestic abuse, in one sitting. This unflinching, filmic sequence of poems illuminates the bleak isolation of the victim, '*who will recover me?*' she asks. It's a terrifying question, set against the familiar settings of a contemporary relationship: the trip away, the picnic, a shared meal. Look at all that is ordinary she says, now let me un-peel the scene.
The trauma and violence in the relationship is evident but so too is the storm-fuse of strength and the fine delicacy of language. Salt is sprinkled as an instrument of pain and cleansing throughout the collection. The anger is palpable and magnificent. '*He will shoot a bird/ right out of the sky if he thinks you heard it/ sing.*' Her poems are golden-threaded with a thick rope of agency and hard-won wisdom. And oh, the beauty and heft of her language:
'*I put aside thoughts of flight*
until in the late pastel light
breeze brought song from familiar cliffs' - **Roz Goddard**

CONTENTS

'And in that year I imagined a vain thing;
I believed that the world would come for me'
Kim Moore

Charles de Gaulle Airport security desk

You will become a victim here.
Collect your bags from the carousel and exit to your right.
Go directly to the accommodation,
hold hands on the sloping staircase
and twist through the narrow doorway to your room.
Take off your shoes and test the mattress.

Remain silent when dragged
from the bed by a fistful of hair
but do enjoy the momentary feeling of weightlessness
as your heels leave the carpet.
Note in particular the exquisite density of the armoire
as it collides with your back.
Do not defend yourself.

Afterwards, sink into the bath,
resenting the city's unnoticing night,
steam melting the ice of your collarbones
as you cry for your mother.

Wait for divers to weave through the wreck of you.
Allow them to sift the detritus of your fingers and knees
until they reveal the circumstances of your breaking.
If offered air, breathe in.

Sleep only in fits and twitches.
When you wake you may be distressed
to see the sun come up,
to hear the clock tick.
You may be shocked to see your eyes
have not swapped places with your ears
and your tongue is still soft.

Our biometric software will not recognise you.
Your loved ones will not vouch for your identity,
send an envoy, or admit to ever having met you.

Do not return to this desk.
Your stay will be indefinite.

i.

did i invoke you
by throwing salt over the wrong shoulder?

Workshop manual for a date

Lay me on a tartan blanket
and crowbar open my ribcage.
Latex-glove your hands
and rummage in my chest
like a giftshop bowl of painted eggs.

Grab your toffee-hammer
and locate organ h1 as shown in the diagram.
Tap the outer shell
until you see a spreading fault line.
Lubricate your wire-cutters
and snip away the brace.
Pour the wine.

Lift out the heart with one hand
and slice it like a bread roll.
Scrape away the darkest cells
with a Stanley knife or similar.
Help yourself to cake
while you perform the cauterisation.
Save me the piece with the most icing.

Refasten my skin to my ribs, buckle
the forks into the basket lid.
Wipe me down with kitchen roll,
blow away the spilled salt
and cool my forehead with a kiss
before gathering your tools to leave.

In the process of recycling, vehicle shells are reduced to fist-sized chunks of metal

We fuck in my car
on your driveway
after a meal out
Later that evening
you kick in the passenger door

Each morning that follows
I push my fingertips
into the gnarled dent
and one day I crash
on the way home from work
and the car gets towed away

I picture metal resisting
the heavy jaws that mangle it
into a neat cube

I wonder

who will recover me and
if I will have my useful
components   removed
before I am compressed
into a convenient shape

Good housekeeping

Lift me up and use me
    Bear heavy on each seam
        I'll brag I'm scorch resistant
            Can absorb your seething steam

           Flatten your crotch against me
        Oh, press me where I stand
    Wrap the cord around my neck
Collapse me with one hand

Improvised weapons found in and around the home

Nottingham Post, 2018: 'Police handing out blunt knives to domestic violence victims to reduce stabbings in the home'.

CD case
Clothes airer
Corded landline telephone
Curtain rail
Dressing gown belt
Fingertips
Front door
Hardback book
Heavy-soled shoe
House key
One of a pair of crutches
Pen
Plate
Trophy
TV remote
Wooden spoon
Water

ii.

a gentle lessening;
one mandolin-thin sliver each day

Scattered
After Roz Goddard

You knew what you were doing
when backs were turned

bruising one petal
and claiming innocence

piercing a stem with your fingernail
so the head would droop as it began to bloom

crushing the flowerbed
in the tread of your boot

then shaking your head at the mess

iii.

damage by seawater or a fine chisel;
cloud the perceived intention

Corrasion

You drew me to ground
homed me with soft nesting
in your upturned hand

safely lofted
and never alone
I put aside thoughts of flight

until in the late pastel light
breeze brought song from familiar cliffs

I unfolded

pushed away on curled feet
breathed in
ready for the lift

but air tore through bare tendon
spun sky & ground twisted me into
a casket of hollow bones

you had plucked one feather every night
whispered
you are not a bird

A butterfly senses her predator

I wait –
pinned in folded symmetry:
these new markings bloom
blacker than the last.

I listen for danger to slip
into the night
before I unclutch my breath
and moment-sleep
in lavender half-light.

Memory fades like an imprint
behind the eyelids
reappearing in a tape-reel.

In the morning
when your waking body turns towards me
my shoulder blades flinch closed
before even your breath
can reach between them.

iv.
slice finely, salt generously;
release of excess moisture and wilting will result

Watermark

hold me up to the light / see the shame / flecked and delicate /
handle me with gloves / easily degraded / cannot be restored / i
like to imagine / getting pulped / starting again / flat and bare

The man is a jealous thief. He will catch you looking at the sunset and close the blinds. He will hear you make plans to visit your sister and put tacks on every inch of road between your houses. He will swagger around your home town smashing every window you ever looked into or out of. He will say *lie* every time your parents tell you they love you. He will _____ you every time he thinks you might love yourself. He will confiscate your phone and replace your fingerprints with his own. He will shoot a bird right out of the sky if he thinks you heard it sing. He will hear you sing and stuff your mouth with _____. He will hide your bank card your car keys and your contraceptive pills. He will change your passwords. He will take the books from your shelves and the art from your walls and leave it all outside overnight in the _____. He will burn your _____ in the kitchen sink. He will empty your box of precious things into the neighbour's skip and you will only find out when you see a photograph of _____ blowing along the road. He will smear your lips with _____ when you speak your friend's name. He will ask you in front of his friends why you are so miserable all the time. He will look at them and laugh and say *after everything I have given her*

18

Means of escape
After William Carlos Williams

she knew
I was on the narrow path
standing alone
in the rain's glaze
waiting for her to make the call

my mouth a cobweb
fists curled in a plea
my fear
a shivering white feather
depending on her to
tell me that she knew

How you will identify my body

Spare key engraved across right palm

Fingerprints on each side of the jaw

look at me when I'm talking to you

Slight spinal curvature indicating bowed head

Tan line on the ring finger of the wrong hand

Fun-house mirror under each eyelid

Scar behind left ear

scream, cry; no-one's listening

Small holes in ventricles consistent with piercing

Alternative names inscribed on the soles of the feet

Indent of hooks around both clavicles

Blunt force injury to the startle reflex

she drove me to it

Knee caps with imprint of hymn book

A birthmark in the shape of a birthmark

You only took photographs of me from the neck down

It is impossible
for a woman with no head
to look you in the eye –
and isn't that just the way you like us?

Conveniently guillotined
from our beach holidays
and your bedroom collection –

A cockroach can live
for nine weeks after its head is removed –

It was fourteen years before I noticed.

v.

a little saline on a teaspoon
offered regularly with the illusion of choice

Mute

silence slips its fingers across my lips
bridles protest to my tongue
pins half-words to my cheek

razored edges of a reversed scream
slice parallel lines into my throat

i gag red on the spill

this riot smoulders
   ignites in a breath
      every rib scorched

next time i'll speak
spew blood and ash

next time i'll speak

Again you fail to turn up dead

I want you to be driving
    and get hit from behind by an articulated lorry
        for the force to lift your wheels from the road
            like a body pushed across a bedroom

I want your steering to be

                powerless

    your braking   impotent

    your screaming   silent

    as a woman crying behind a window

I want you to wonder

    if   anyone will help you
    if   you will return to the ground
    how

you let it happen

Happiness is not the same

as the relief of being yanked free
from a bathroom window
as flames engulf the house

vi.
steep the skin in a warm salt bath;
excavate carefully with a needle

Trauma kit

a lamp to expose it
a fence to prevent it
an ocean to drown it

a potion to daub on the lintel
a mirror to see it coming
a tripwire to slow its approach

a sigil to sketch on our chests
a note to share under desks
a sign to say don't fall in

a tool to extract it
a balm to soothe it
a spell to reverse it

Learning from Nigella Lawson

Soften onions in oil on a low flame
watch them sweat and become translucent.
Reflect on the last time you felt scared.

Add chilli, ginger and lemongrass
let the heat release the fragrance.
Know that you won't hear *what is that shit?*
shouted from another room.

Spoon in green curry paste – your own or from a jar.
Relax it with a drop of coconut milk.
Think about the first time you felt safe.

Add a variety of vegetables
move them around the pan until coated.
Move your bare feet around the floor – feel free to dance.

Now, delicate leaves of pak choi
podded edamame, or both.
Please yourself.

Pour the rest of the coconut milk freely
sweet as from your own breast.
Bring to a gentle simmer.
Take a deep and whole breath.

Check the rice has absorbed the water it needs.
Contemplate what absorbed you
and when you disappeared.

Serve yourself with what you have made
brighten with lime, scatter coriander.
This meal will not be thrown against the kitchen wall.
You will not be thrown against the kitchen wall.

Pour a drink – wine, or water.
Sit and eat.

Acknowledgements

Thank you to the editors of the following journals and anthologies in which earlier versions of some of these poems have appeared: *Away With Words, Anthropocene, Whirlagust (Yaffle Prize 2019 Anthology), Finished Creatures, Algebra of Owls, Lemon Curd,* and *100 Voices.*

'Scattered' takes inspiration from a line in *This Poem is For You* by Roz Goddard, published in *#MeToo*, an anthology edited by Deborah Alma (Fair Acre Press 2018).

'Means of escape' takes inspiration from *The Red Wheelbarrow* by William Carlos Williams, published in *The Collected Poems: Volume I 1909-1939* (New Directions Publishing Corporation, 1938).

The title of 'In the process of recycling, vehicle shells are reduced to fist-sized chunks of metal' is taken directly from the Wikipedia entry for *Vehicle Recycling* (https://en.wikipedia.org/wiki/Vehicle_recycling).

'Learning from Nigella Lawson' won the 2019 Creative Future Writers' Award Gold Prize for Poetry.

Thank you to my dear friend Jo, who encouraged me early on not only to write but to submit for publication, and who continues to be my biggest cheerleader. Deep gratitude and thanks to my friend and mentor Nellie Cole, who kickstarted and empowered my poetry journey. Thank you to Liam Bates for kindly providing feedback on an early version of the manuscript. Thank you to my ever supportive parents who have helped me in countless ways to enable this pamphlet to be written. Thank you to my wonderful daughters for always being supportive of my work and giving me reason to write. Thank you to all those who have shown love and support along the way.

Thank you to Scarlett Ward Bennett at Fawn Press for her friendship and encouragement, for having faith in these poems and for the editing suggestions that brought the pamphlet together.